W9-BUP-540

A Little
San Francisco
Cookbook

Charlotte Walker

Illustrated by Brenda Rae Eno

Chronicle Books · San Francisco

Copyright © 1990 by Chronicle Books. All rights reserved.
No part of this book may be reproduced in any form without
written permission from the publisher.

Printed in Singapore

10   9   8   7   6   5   4   3   2

ISBN: 0-87701-619-4

Chronicle Books
275 Fifth Street
San Francisco, California   94103

CONTENTS

Soups
Fisherman's
Wharf Cioppino 4

Salads
California Caesar Salad 6
Wild Rice Salad 9
Golden Gate Pasta
Salad 10
Smoked Chicken and
Apple Salad 13
Crab Louis 14

Appetizers
Dragon Chicken in
Lettuce Leaves 16
South-of-Market
Salsa 19

Sandwiches
Vivande's Eggplant
Sandwiches 20
Aram Sandwiches 22
Balboa Blue Cheese
Burgers 25
Italian Stacked
Sandwich 26

Grains
Mission Rice 29

Main Dishes
Wine Country Lamb on
Skewers 31
Hangtown Fry 32
Chardonnay Shrimp 35
Joe's Special 37
North Beach Pasta with
Italian Sausage and
Tomato Sauce 38
Sausages and Peppers
with Creamy Polenta 41
City Pizza 42

Breads
San Francisco
Sourdough Bread 47
Peppery Olive
Focaccia 53

Desserts
Ginger-Almond
Cookies 55
San Francisco Irish
Coffee 57
Ghirardelli Gay Nineties
Silk Pie 59

Fisherman's Wharf Cioppino

Fishermen of Italian and Portuguese descent created cioppino, a hearty tomato-based stew redolent of garlic and herbs and rich with the day's catch. Italian dried mushrooms (porcini), available in specialty stores and many supermarkets, give this version a satisfying earthy flavor. Serve it with plenty of crusty bread to soak up the broth.

1½ ounces dried Italian mushrooms
¼ cup olive oil
1 large onion, chopped
4 garlic cloves, minced
1 large green bell pepper, cored, seeded, and chopped
4 large tomatoes, peeled, seeded, and chopped
½ cup canned tomato purée
2 cups fish stock or bottled clam juice
2 cups dry white wine
2 tablespoons minced fresh parsley
2 tablespoons minced fresh basil or
1½ teaspoons dried basil
Salt, ground black pepper, and sugar to taste
2 to 2½ pounds Dungeness crab, cleaned and cracked
18 small or medium hard-shell clams, scrubbed
1 pound firm-textured skinless fish fillets, cut into
1½- to 2-inch pieces
1 pound medium shrimp, peeled and deveined

Thoroughly rinse mushrooms. In a small bowl, cover rinsed mushrooms with warm water; soak 20 minutes, or until soft and pliable. Squeeze mushrooms dry and strain soaking liquid through several layers of cheesecloth; set aside. Coarsely chop soaked mushrooms; set aside. Heat oil in a large kettle. Add onion and garlic; sauté until soft. Add green pepper; cook 5 minutes longer. Add tomatoes, tomato puree, fish stock, wine, parsley, and basil. Add 3 to

4 tablespoons reserved strained mushroom liquid. Add salt, pepper, and sugar to taste. Cover and simmer 20 minutes. Broth can be made ahead to this point and refrigerated 6 to 8 hours.

At serving time, bring broth to a simmer. Add crab pieces; cover and cook 3 to 5 minutes. Add clams and fish pieces; cover and simmer 5 minutes longer. Add shrimp. Cook until shrimp become firm and turn pink, and clams open, 3 to 5 minutes. *(Discard any clams that do not open.)* Serve from kettle or spoon into a tureen. Makes 6 servings.

California Caesar Salad

Sun-dried tomatoes marinated in olive oil give a contemporary twist to the classic Caesar salad.

Garlic Croutons, following
2 garlic cloves
One 2-ounce can anchovies, drained
½ cup olive oil
¼ cup freshly squeezed lemon juice
½ teaspoon Dijon-style mustard
½ teaspoon Worcestershire sauce
Coarsely ground black pepper to taste
Leaves from 1 head romaine lettuce, washed and dried
½ cup drained marinated sun-dried tomatoes, oil reserved
¼ cup freshly grated Parmesan cheese

Prepare Garlic Croutons; set aside. To prepare dressing, purée garlic and anchovies in a blender or a food processor. Add oil, lemon juice, mustard, and Worcestershire sauce; blend thoroughly. Season with pepper. Gently tear lettuce into a salad bowl. Top with Garlic Croutons, tomatoes, and cheese. Drizzle with dressing. Toss and serve immediately. Makes 4 to 6 servings.

Garlic Croutons: In a skillet over medium heat, warm 3 tablespoons of the oil from sun-dried tomatoes and 2 chopped garlic cloves. Add 3 cups ½-inch bread cubes; toss to coat. Transfer in a single layer to a baking sheet. Bake in a preheated 325° oven, tossing occasionally, until crisp and golden, about 12 to 15 minutes. Cool.

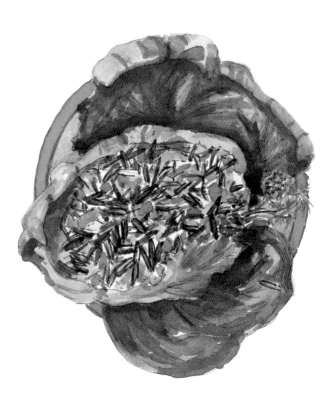

Wild Rice Salad

One of California's newest crops is wild rice, grown in the Yuba City area northeast of San Francisco. Technically, wild rice is an aquatic grain that resembles wheat more closely than rice.

Mustard-Thyme Vinaigrette, following
1 cup wild rice (4 to 4½ cups cooked)
8 ounces diced smoked chicken or ham
1 large tart green apple, diced
1 medium red bell pepper, cut into ¼-inch squares
½ cup sliced green onions
3 tablespoons minced fresh parsley
Red cabbage or kale

Prepare vinaigrette; set aside. Cook wild rice according to package directions; cool to room temperature. In a bowl, toss together all ingredients, except cabbage, with dressing. Serve on a bed of red cabbage. Makes 5 to 6 servings.

Mustard-Thyme Vinaigrette: Combine 3 tablespoons apple cider vinegar, 3 tablespoons German-style mustard or Dijon mustard, 1 minced garlic clove, 1 teaspoon dried thyme leaves, 1 teaspoon sugar, ½ teaspoon salt, and ½ teaspoon pepper. Beat in ⅓ cup light olive oil.

Golden Gate Pasta Salad

Each September San Franciscans are hosted by the San Francisco Opera to a day-long performance of opera in Golden Gate Park. It's a good day to pack a picnic that includes this pasta salad.

8 ounces pasta, such as whole-wheat spaghetti,
bow-tie, or corkscrew-shaped pasta
4 ounces snow peas, trimmed and cooked tender-crisp
4 ounces enoki mushrooms or
sliced small button mushrooms
½ cup sliced pitted black olives

Dressing

¼ cup sun-dried tomatoes, drained and minced
2 garlic cloves, minced
2 cups packed fresh basil leaves, minced
1 cup (4 ounces) freshly grated Parmesan cheese
3 tablespoons red wine vinegar
¾ teaspoon salt
¼ teaspoon ground black pepper
¾ cup olive oil
1½ pounds tomatoes, peeled, seeded, and minced
6 ounces feta cheese, crumbled

Cook pasta until al dente in a large quantity of boiling salted water. Drain; rinse in cold water; drain again and place in a bowl. Cut snow peas in half; add to pasta with mushrooms and olives; toss to combine. To make the dressing: In a bowl, combine sun-dried tomatoes, garlic, basil, Parmesan cheese, vinegar, salt, and pepper. Whisk in olive oil. Stir in tomatoes. (Dressing can be easily prepared in a food processor fitted with a metal blade: Mince sun-dried tomatoes and garlic. Add basil and Parmesan cheese; process until coarsely ground. Add tomatoes and pulse 3 or 4 times until chopped, but not puréed.) Pour dressing over pasta and toss. Sprinkle with feta cheese. (Salad can be prepared a day ahead of serving.) Makes 6 servings as a first course.

~~~~

Smoked Chicken and Apple Salad

Smoked chicken is one of the most popular ingredients in contemporary California cuisine.

Orange-Ginger Dressing, following
4 cups shredded smoked chicken
1 small red apple and 1 tart green apple, diced
½ cup sliced green onions
⅔ cup chopped toasted walnuts

Garnish

1 red apple, cored and sliced crosswise into thin circles
2 kiwis, peeled and sliced thin
4 to 5 large fresh mint leaves, shredded

Prepare dressing; set aside. Combine chicken, apples, green onions, and walnuts in a bowl; toss with dressing. To serve, overlap apple and kiwi slices on one side of each of 5 or 6 serving plates. Mound chicken mixture to the side of fruit. Sprinkle with shredded mint.

Orange-Ginger Dressing: Combine 1 cup mayonnaise, 1 cup plain yogurt, 1 tablespoon grated fresh ginger, 2 teaspoons grated fresh orange peel, ¼ cup freshly squeezed orange juice, and ¼ teaspoon salt.

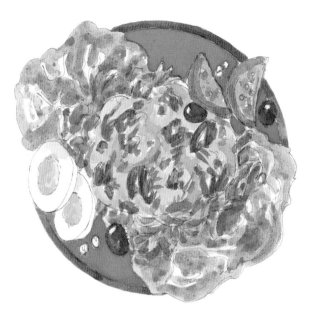

Crab Louis

This classic salad originated in San Francisco, and every wharfside restaurant features its own version. Tiny shelled shrimp, called bay shrimp in San Francisco, can be substituted for crab.

Louis Dressing, following
1 head iceberg lettuce
¾ to 1 pound cooked crabmeat, shredded
2 medium tomatoes, cut in wedges
2 hard-cooked eggs, cut in wedges
Capers
Black olives

Prepare Louis Dressing; cover and refrigerate at least 1 hour to let flavors blend. Rinse, core, and drain lettuce. Place 1 large lettuce leaf on each of 4 plates. Shred remaining lettuce to make 6 cups. (Refrigerate any remaining lettuce for another use.) Place shredded lettuce on lettuce leaves. Arrange crabmeat evenly over it. Spoon about half of the dressing over crabmeat. Garnish each plate with tomato wedges, egg wedges, capers, and olives. Serve remaining dressing separately. Makes 4 servings.

Louis Dressing

½ cup mayonnaise
½ cup sour cream
3 to 4 tablespoons tomato-based chili sauce
1 tablespoon fresh lemon juice
Few drops hot-pepper sauce
¼ cup finely diced green bell pepper
¼ cup finely sliced green onions

Combine ingredients in a small bowl; blend well.

Dragon Chicken in Lettuce Leaves

The original Cantonese dish uses squab, which is expensive and hard to find, and therefore is reserved for festive occasions. Substitute chicken and you can easily make this recipe for more casual gatherings.

Marinade

2 tablespoons soy sauce   2 tablespoons dry sherry
1 teaspoon sugar   2 garlic cloves, minced
2 teaspoons grated fresh ginger
⅛ teaspoon hot red pepper flakes (optional)

1 medium head iceberg lettuce
2 boned and skinned chicken breast halves (¾ pound)
One 8-ounce can water chestnuts, drained
3 green onions   ⅓ cup chicken broth or water
2 teaspoons cornstarch dissolved in 2 tablespoons water
2 teaspoons sesame oil
2 tablespoons chopped fresh cilantro

Mix together marinade ingredients in a large bowl; reserve. Tear large leaves in half or thirds; set aside. Finely chop chicken, water chestnuts, and green onions separately with a heavy knife or in a food processor. Stir into marinade.

Heat oil in a large wok or frying pan. Add chicken mixture; stir-fry until chicken is opaque, 3 to 5 minutes. Add chicken broth and cornstarch mixture. Cook over medium heat, stirring constantly, until cornstarch thickens. Stir in sesame oil. Mound chicken mixture in center of a platter. Sprinkle with cilantro. Surround chicken mixture with about 20 lettuce leaves. To eat, place 2 tablespoons chicken mixture in a lettuce leaf; roll up. Makes 4 to 6 servings.

South-of-Market Salsa

The city is always lively south of Market Street. This snappy salsa combines the colors, flavors, and smells of the Mission District's Latin American markets.

2 cups chopped seeded tomatoes
2 green onions, tops included, chopped
2 garlic cloves, minced
1 teaspoon or more minced fresh hot chili peppers, such as jalapeño or serrano chilies
1 tablespoon olive oil or vegetable oil
2 teaspoons or more freshly squeezed lime juice
8 to 10 sprigs cilantro, minced
Salt to taste

In a medium bowl, stir together tomatoes, green onions, garlic, chili peppers, oil, lime juice, and cilantro. Season with salt. Adjust flavors to taste, adding more chilies and lime juice, if desired. Makes about 2 cups.

Vivande's Eggplant Sandwiches

This is one of the most popular and unusual sandwiches on the menu at Vivande Porta Via on Fillmore Street in San Francisco. Carlo Middione features this recipe in his book *The Food of Southern Italy*. He cautions that some of the provolone may melt and flow out onto the baking sheet. "Just scrape it off," he says, "and eat it when no one is looking."

¼ cup olive oil
1 medium eggplant (about 1¼ pounds), cut into twelve
½-inch-thick rounds
½ teaspoon salt
¼ teaspoon pepper
6 thin slices (4 ounces) provolone cheese
6 thin slices (4 ounces) mortadella
⅓ cup dry bread crumbs
⅓ cup freshly grated Parmesan cheese
¼ cup minced fresh parsley
2 large eggs
2 tablespoons water

Heat oven to 350°. Brush a 15½-by-10½-inch baking pan with 2 tablespoons of the oil. Sprinkle eggplant slices with salt and pepper. Top each of 6 slices with a slice of provolone and a slice of mortadella (fold or tear to fit). Cover with a slice of eggplant. Mix bread crumbs, Parmesan cheese, and parsley in a shallow dish. In a separate dish beat eggs with water. Dip each sandwich into egg mixture, then into crumb mixture, scooping crumbs onto top and sides and pressing firmly to coat well. Arrange in prepared pan. Drizzle 1 teaspoon oil over each. Bake, turning once, for 35 to 40 minutes, or until eggplant is golden and tender when pierced. Makes 6 sandwiches.

Aram Sandwiches

These sandwiches were first popularized by the Caravansary restaurant. The big bubbly rounds of crisp Armenian cracker bread, also known as *lavosh*, are rolled up like a jelly roll, enclosing the filling. When the roll is cut, it makes pinwheel sandwiches that are perfect for hors d'oeuvres, light meals, and picnics.

1 round Armenian cracker bread, 14 to 16 inches in diameter

Roast Beef, Tomato, and Lettuce Filling

One 3-ounce package cream cheese, at room temperature
1 tablespoon prepared horseradish or Dijon mustard
About 1 tablespoon water
6 ounces very thinly sliced roast beef
2 small tomatoes, sliced very thin
2 loosely packed cups shredded lettuce

To soften cracker bread, hold under a gentle stream of cold tap water for about 10 seconds per side until well moistened. Place flat between damp clean kitchen towels. (If working with more than 1 round of bread, stack with a damp towel between layers.) Let stand about 1 hour, or until bread is soft and pliable. Check during standing time; if bread is crisp in spots, sprinkle with additional water.

To make filling mixture, beat cream cheese in a small bowl until light. Beat in horseradish or mustard, then enough water so mixture is of spreading consistency.

To assemble, spread cheese mixture over 1 side of bread to within ¼ inch of edge. Layer beef, tomatoes, and lettuce over cheese mixture, overlapping meat slightly if necessary. Roll up tight, jelly-roll style. Wrap in plastic wrap and refrigerate at least 1 hour or up to 2 days. To serve, trim ends with a serrated knife, then cut roll into 12 thick slices. Makes 6 servings (2 slices each).

Ham, Cucumber, and Sprouts Variation: Prepare sandwiches as in the preceding recipe, using the following filling: One 3-ounce package cream cheese, at room temperature; 1 tablespoon minced fresh dill or 1 teaspoon dried dill; about 1 tablespoon fresh lemon juice; 6 ounces very thinly sliced cooked ham; 1 medium cucumber, peeled and sliced very thin; 1 cup alfalfa spouts.

~~~~

Balboa Blue Cheese Burgers

The Balboa Cafe on Fillmore Street serves up some of the best burgers in town. This rendition is named in its honor.

2 pounds lean ground beef
2 garlic cloves, minced
1 teaspoon salt
½ teaspoon ground black pepper
4 ounces blue cheese
⅓ cup chopped walnuts
1 long baguette
Olive oil
Chopped fresh parsley

Heat oven to 500°. Combine beef, garlic, salt, and pepper. Shape meat into 12 oval patties. Mash cheese and blend with walnuts. Divide cheese mixture equally onto centers of 6 patties. Top with remaining patties, pinching edges together to seal in filling. Place on a baking sheet and bake 10 to 12 minutes, or to desired doneness. (Burgers can be pan fried or charcoal grilled, too.) Cut baguette into 6 pieces; split each piece and paint with olive oil. Place on a baking sheet and toast at 500° for 3 to 4 minutes. Sprinkle burgers with chopped parsley. Makes 6 servings.

Italian Stacked Sandwich

Bands of colorful ingredients create a striking appearance
when this sandwich is cut.

1 round loaf Italian bread, about 9 inches in diameter
1 bunch (about 4 ounces) watercress
1 garlic clove, minced
One 2-ounce can anchovy fillets, drained
3 green onions, chopped
1 teaspoon dried oregano
3 tablespoons fresh lemon juice
$2/3$ cup olive oil
1 cup sliced black olives
One 4-ounce jar pimientos, drained
4 ounces each thinly sliced salami, provolone, and
mortadella

Split loaf horizontally and remove soft interior bread from loaf, leaving a shell ½ to ¾ inch thick. Tear interior apart to make 1½ cups bread pieces; reserve. Remove watercress leaves from stems; discard stems. Place half of the watercress leaves, garlic, anchovy fillets, green onions, oregano, lemon juice, and bread crumbs in a food processor or blender. Process, pulsing off and on, until ingredients are ground. With the motor running, add olive oil in a steady stream. Spread dressing on inside of bread shells. Place half of the olives, pimientos, and remaining watercress leaves in bottom shell of bread. Layer on salami, provolone, and mortadella. Mound on remaining watercress, pimientos, and olives. Cover with top shell and press sandwich together. Wrap sandwich in foil and let stand at least 30 minutes. Cut sandwich into wedges. Makes 6 servings.

Mission Rice

This dish represents the colorful Hispanic district of San Francisco called the Mission.

4 ounces bulk chorizo sausage
½ cup minced onion
1 cup raw long-grain rice
1¾ cups chicken broth
¼ cup tomato purée
½ teaspoon salt
1 cup frozen tiny peas, thawed
1 small ripe avocado, peeled and sliced

In a skillet, brown sausage, breaking it up with a fork until it is cooked through. Remove sausage and drain most fat from pan. Add onions; cook 5 minutes or until soft. Add rice and cook, stirring, 5 minutes longer. Return drained sausage to pan. Add broth, tomato purée, and salt. Bring to a boil. Lower heat, cover, and simmer for 25 minutes, or until rice is tender and liquid is absorbed. Stir in peas. Let rest, covered, for 5 minutes. Garnish platter or individual servings with avocado slices. Makes 6 servings.

Wine Country Lamb on Skewers

A California Pinot Noir or Zinfandel is the perfect wine for marinating and serving with grilled lamb.

½ cup dry red wine
¼ cup olive oil
2 garlic cloves, slivered
½ teaspoon each dried thyme, rosemary, and salt
¼ teaspoon ground black pepper
2 pounds boneless lamb, cut from shoulder or leg

In a non-aluminum baking dish or bowl, combine wine, oil, garlic, and seasonings. Trim and cut lamb into 1-inch cubes. Add to marinade; marinate lamb at room temperature for 2 to 4 hours, or cover and refrigerate for up to 24 hours. Light a fire in a grill or heat a broiler. Thread lamb onto each of 8 wooden or metal skewers. (If using wooden skewers, first soak in water for at least 15 minutes.) Grill over low coals, or broil, turning several times, for about 10 minutes, or to desired doneness. Makes 4 servings.

Hangtown Fry

During the Gold Rush, Placerville, California, was known as Hangtown, a name no doubt derived from Western justice. As the story goes, Hangtown Fry was created when a miner who'd struck it rich ordered up a dish worth its weight in gold. Since eggs and bacon were scarce and terribly expensive, and oysters had to be shipped in from the east, the creation became a legend.

One 8- or 10-ounce jar shucked oysters, drained
Salt and pepper to taste
All-purpose flour for dredging
10 eggs
1 tablespoon water
¾ cup finely crushed saltine crackers
¼ cup milk
½ teaspoon salt
¼ teaspoon ground pepper
3 tablespoons butter
12 to 15 crisp-fried bacon slices (3 per person)

If oysters are large, cut in half. Season lightly with salt and pepper. Roll each oyster in flour to coat lightly. In a shallow dish, beat 1 egg with 1 tablespoon water. Dip oysters in egg mixture, then roll in cracker crumbs to coat. In a medium bowl, beat together remaining eggs, milk, ½ teaspoon salt, and ¼ teaspoon pepper.

To make 2 omelettes: For each omelette, melt half the butter in a 10-inch skillet. Add half the coated oysters; brown quickly on both sides over medium-high heat. (Be careful not to overcook.) Pour half the egg mixture over oysters in skillet. Reduce heat to low; cook until egg mixture is set. During cooking, lift cooked egg mixture with a spatula and let uncooked egg mixture run underneath. To serve, fold omelette in half; turn out onto a platter. Repeat with remaining mixture.

Chardonnay Shrimp

The Napa and Sonoma valleys, about an hour and a half's drive north of San Francisco, are wine-producing areas famous for Chardonnay wine. The buttery taste of Chardonnay is a natural pairing with shrimp, and this recipe leaves plenty in the bottle to be enjoyed along with the meal. Serve the dish with French bread to soak up the cooking juices.

½ cup butter
2 garlic cloves, minced
1 cup Chardonnay or other dry white wine
1 teaspoon Worcestershire sauce
½ teaspoon each salt, dried thyme, and dried oregano
¼ teaspoon or more hot red pepper flakes, crushed
1½ pounds in-shell medium shrimp, rinsed
2 tablespoons minced fresh parsley

Melt butter in a large skillet over medium heat. Add garlic; cook 1 minute. Stir in wine, Worcestershire sauce, and seasonings; bring to a boil. Add shrimp; simmer 4 to 5 minutes until firm and pink, stirring frequently. Sprinkle with parsley. Serve shrimp in wide shallow bowls with cooking juices. Makes 4 servings.

Joe's Special

No one has to tell a San Franciscan about Joe's Special: a late-night conglomeration of ground beef, spinach, eggs, and seasonings. It was made famous by the first Original Joe's restaurant, located on Broadway. Everyone has a slight twist on the original; here's one version.

1 pound ground beef
1 small onion, diced
1 teaspoon dried Italian seasonings blend
1 teaspoon salt
¼ teaspoon ground black pepper
One 10-ounce package frozen chopped spinach, thawed
and squeezed dry
4 eggs, slightly beaten

Brown ground beef in a large skillet, breaking it up until crumbly. Drain grease from pan. Add onion and cook until tender but not browned. Stir in Italian seasonings, salt, and pepper. Stir in spinach; cook and stir until any liquid in spinach has evaporated. Add eggs to meat mixture and cook, stirring, until eggs are set. Makes 4 servings.

North Beach Pasta
with Italian Sausage and
Tomato Sauce

When Italians settled in the North Beach area of San
Francisco, they brought their robust old-country recipes.

1½ pounds mild and/or hot fresh Italian sausage,
cut into ¾-inch pieces
1 large onion, thinly sliced
3 large garlic cloves, minced
One 28-ounce can peeled whole tomatoes
⅓ cup Marsala wine
¼ cup chopped fresh basil, or 3 tablespoons chopped fresh
parsley plus 2 teaspoons dried basil
Salt and freshly ground pepper to taste
12 ounces spaghetti

Brown sausage over medium-high heat in a heavy wide-bottomed pan or a skillet with high sides. Remove sausage from pan. Add onion and garlic; sauté in sausage fat for about 2 minutes. Pour off excess grease. Remove tomatoes from can; drain and coarsely chop, reserving juice. Return sausage to pan; add tomatoes, Marsala, and about ½ of the juice from can. (If using dried basil, add it now.) Cook sauce over medium heat for 10 minutes to evaporate some of the liquid. Stir in fresh basil or parsley. Season with salt and pepper. Cook spaghetti according to package directions. Use sauce immediately on the pasta or cool to room temperature and refrigerate or freeze. Makes 4 servings.

Sausages and Peppers with Creamy Polenta

Serve up tall glasses of Anchor Steam beer with this savory dish. Fritz Maytag, brewmeister of the Anchor Brewing Company, has been making specialty beers in San Francisco since the 1960s.

Polenta

5 cups chicken broth
1 cup Italian polenta (coarse yellow cornmeal)
1 cup water
Salt and freshly ground black pepper to taste
½ cup heavy cream
2 tablespoons butter

2 pounds sweet or hot fresh Italian sausage links,
cut into 1½-inch pieces
1 large onion, sliced and separated into rings
2 medium red bell peppers, cored, seeded, and
cut into thin strips
2 garlic cloves, minced
⅓ cup Marsala, medium-sweet Madeira, or
sweet vermouth

Finely shredded fresh basil or chopped fresh parsley
Freshly grated Parmesan cheese

Bring chicken broth to a boil in a large saucepan. In a medium bowl, stir polenta into water. Pour water and polenta into boiling chicken broth. Cook at a gentle boil, stirring frequently, for about 30 minutes. Season with salt and pepper. Remove pot from heat; stir in cream and butter, and keep warm over very low heat.

Meanwhile, during last 10 minutes of cooking polenta, in a large skillet, brown sausage over medium heat until cooked through. Remove from pan; set aside. Pour all but 1 tablespoon of fat from pan. Add onion; cook over medium-high heat for 1 to 2 minutes. Add peppers and garlic; cook several minutes more until vegetables are tender-crisp. Return sausage to pan. Add Marsala and cook over high heat, stirring constantly, until some liquid has evaporated. Sprinkle with fresh herbs. Place polenta and sausages on separate platters. Serve family style. Pass Parmesan cheese at the table. Makes 6 servings.

~~~~~

City Pizza

A continuing debate among North Beach residents concerns which style of pizza crust is best: thin and crisp, or

thick and chewy? This pizza may not end the debate, but it seems to suit many tastes.

Dough

2¾ cups unbleached all-purpose flour
½ cup yellow cornmeal
1 package (2 teaspoons) active dry yeast
1 tablespoon sugar
1 teaspoon salt
¾ cup hot (105° to 110°) water
3 tablespoons olive oil

Topping

One 28-ounce can whole peeled tomatoes
1½ teaspoons each dried basil and oregano leaves
1 large garlic clove, minced
¼ teaspoon ground black pepper
¾ pound mozzarella cheese, thinly sliced
6 ounces thinly sliced salami or pepperoni
½ cup (2 ounces) freshly grated Parmesan cheese

In a food processor fitted with a plastic dough blade, process flour, cornmeal, yeast, sugar, and salt to blend. With motor running, add water and oil in a steady stream. Process until mixture comes away from sides of work bowl. Process 1 minute to knead dough. If dough is sticky, add more flour. Process 30 to 60 seconds longer. Dough should feel tacky, smooth, elastic, and warm, but not hot. Remove dough from processor and shape into a ball. Or, combine ingredients in a large bowl using a wooden spoon; turn out onto a floured board and knead for 5 to 8 minutes, or until smooth and elastic; form into a ball. Place dough in a large oiled bowl; turn to coat it with oil. Cover bowl with plastic wrap or a damp towel. Let dough rise until doubled in bulk, 30 to 60 minutes.

Heat oven to 475°. Punch dough down. Roll or pat it to fit a greased 14-inch-round deep-dish pizza pan or 10-by-15-inch jelly-roll pan. Ease dough into pan, pushing it up about 1 inch around edge. Prick bottom and sides with a fork. Bake 7 minutes to set crust; remove from oven to a cooling rack. (Crust can be prepared to this point and held at room temperature for up to 24 hours before finishing pizza, or it can be frozen for up to 2 months.)

To finish pizza, drain juice from canned tomatoes. Squeeze tomatoes to remove seeds and excess liquid, and break up into small bits. Combine tomatoes, basil, oregano, garlic, and pepper. Arrange mozzarella cheese on dough. Spread tomato mixture on top. Top with salami or pepperoni. Sprinkle on Parmesan cheese. Bake 20 to 30 minutes, or until crust is browned. Makes 8 slices.

San Francisco Sourdough Bread

Thanks to the Gold Rush, sourdough bread is a specialty of San Francisco. The prospectors learned that saving some of the yeasty batter, "the mother," for the next day's baking provided a continuous supply of bread.

Nothing beats the tangy flavor and chewy crust of sourdough bread. The loaves often are made plump and round, with the top crust scored in a tic-tac-toe shape. But you can form the dough into any shape, from long baguettes to individual rolls.

1 package (2 teaspoons) active dry yeast
1 tablespoon sugar
2 cups warm (105° to 115°) water
2 teaspoons salt
1 cup Sourdough Starter, following, at room temperature
2 cups bread flour
5 to 5½ cups unbleached all-purpose flour
Cornmeal for sprinkling
1 egg white mixed with 1 tablespoon water, for glaze

In a large bowl, dissolve yeast and sugar in ½ cup of the warm water. Stir in remaining water, salt, and starter. Add bread flour and 2 cups of the all-purpose flour. Mix to blend. Beat by hand or with an electric beater until smooth and elastic, about 5 minutes. Gradually beat in 2 to 2½ cups all-purpose flour to make a stiff dough. Turn dough onto a lightly floured surface and knead for 10 to 15 minutes, or until smooth and elastic. Knead in only enough remaining flour to prevent the dough from being too sticky. (It should feel tacky, not dry.) Form into a ball, place in a greased bowl, and turn to coat. Cover and let rise in a warm place until doubled in bulk, 1 to 1½ hours.

Punch dough down, cover with an inverted bowl, and let rest 10 minutes. Divide into 2 equal portions. Shape each into a disc and place on greased baking sheets that have been sprinkled with cornmeal. Let rise until doubled again, 1 to 1½ hours. Preheat oven to 400°. With a razor blade, slash tops of loaves three ways horizontally and three ways vertically in a tic-tac-toe design. Brush with egg white glaze. Bake for 15 minutes; brush with glaze again. Bake 15 to 20 minutes more, or until loaves are golden and sound hollow when tapped. Cool on wire racks. Makes 2 loaves.

Sourdough Starter

1 package (2 teaspoons) active dry yeast
1 tablespoon sugar
1 cup warm (105° to 115°) water
1 cup warm (105° to 115°) nonfat milk
2 cups unbleached all-purpose flour

In a large nonmetal container or bowl, dissolve yeast and sugar in warm water. Stir in milk. Add flour; mix to blend, then beat until smooth. (Small lumps will dissolve in the fermentation process.) Cover container with 2 or 3 layers of cheesecloth; secure with a rubber band. Let stand in a warm place (75° to 85°) for 2 to 4 days, stirring mixture several times a day, until it has a pleasant sour aroma and is full of bubbles. Refrigerate until ready to use. To use, bring to room temperature, about 1–2 hours, and stir down starter before measuring it. After each use, replenish as directed below.

The Care and Feeding of a Sourdough Starter:

- Make the sourdough starter several days before you plan to bake to allow the starter to ferment properly.
- Start with a large enough container to allow the mixture to double in bulk. Use glass, earthenware, or plastic containers, not metal.
- Replenish the starter using equal parts of flour and warm (105° to 115°) nonfat milk. If you've used 1 cup of starter in the recipe, blend in 1 cup *each* of flour and warm milk. Then cover the starter and let it stand in a warm place several hours or overnight until it's active and bubbly.
- Refrigerate the starter between uses in a tightly covered container. Bring it to room temperature before using it.
- Starters will last indefinitely if you use them regularly, every 10 to 14 days. If you don't use the starter for 2 to 3 weeks, remove ½ cup and discard, then replenish it as directed above. This will keep the starter going.

Peppery Olive Focaccia

Several bakeries in North Beach offer versions of this traditional trattoria bread, which can be made easily at home with frozen bread dough.

Two 1-pound loaves frozen bread dough, thawed
2 tablespoons extra-virgin olive oil
2 garlic cloves, minced
⅛ to ¼ teaspoon hot red pepper flakes, crushed
1 teaspoon minced fresh rosemary, or
½ teaspoon crumbled dried rosemary
⅓ cup chopped pitted olives
½ cup freshly grated Parmesan cheese

Lightly oil a 10-by-15-inch jelly-roll pan. Pat and stretch dough to fit bottom of pan. Drizzle with olive oil. Sprinkle on garlic, red pepper flakes, rosemary, olives, and Parmesan cheese. Let rise at room temperature for 1 hour. Bake at 375° for 12 to 15 minutes, or until browned. Cut into squares. Makes 8 to 12 servings.

Ginger-Almond Cookies

Almond cookies and sweet custard tartlettes dot the bakeries of San Francisco's Chinatown. This cookie is especially good made with fresh ginger, a staple Chinese ingredient.

¾ cup butter, at room temperature
1 cup packed dark brown sugar
2 tablespoons light molasses
1 egg
1 tablespoon finely grated fresh ginger, or
1¼ teaspoons ground ginger
2¼ cups unbleached all-purpose flour
1½ teaspoons baking powder
½ teaspoon salt
About 48 whole blanched almonds

In a large bowl, cream butter and brown sugar until light and fluffy. Beat in molasses, egg, and ginger. Combine flour, baking powder, and salt. Mix dry ingredients into butter-sugar mixture until completely blended. Wrap dough in plastic wrap and refrigerate several hours. Heat oven to 350°. Form dough into walnut-sized balls and place 2 inches apart on greased cookie sheets. Press an almond into center of each ball. Bake for 10 to 12 minutes, or until lightly browned on bottom. Makes about 4 dozen.

San Francisco Irish Coffee

On nights when the foghorns bellow, there's nothing like ending the evening with an Irish coffee. It's a tradition that attracts locals and tourists alike to the Buena Vista Cafe along Fisherman's Wharf.

1¼ ounces Irish whiskey
Hot strong coffee
Sugar cubes (optional)
Whipped cream

Combine whiskey and hot coffee in a 6-ounce glass. Add sugar to taste and stir to dissolve. Top with whipped cream. Makes 1 serving.

Ghirardelli Gay Nineties Silk Pie

The Ghirardelli family of San Francisco established one of the world's finest chocolate companies in 1852. Today a Ghirardelli confectionary shop still stands in San Francisco's historic Ghirardelli Square. Silk Pie is a recipe from their culinary collection.

Crust

4 ounces (4 squares) bittersweet chocolate
1 cup coarsely chopped pecans
½ cup packed brown sugar
1 tablespoon butter, cut up

Filling

1 cup butter, softened
1½ cups sifted powdered sugar
3 eggs, well beaten
2 tablespoons bourbon whiskey
8 ounces (8 squares) bittersweet chocolate
¼ cup heavy cream

White Laced Whipped Cream, following

Break chocolate into small pieces and combine with remaining ingredients in a blender or food processor; process for 20 seconds, or until crumbly. (If a blender is used, blend chocolate first, then add remaining ingredients.) Press crumbs into a 9-inch pie plate. Chill while preparing filling.

To make filling, cream butter with sugar until fluffy. Beat in eggs and bourbon. Break chocolate into small pieces. In a heavy saucepan, melt broken chocolate with cream, stirring constantly. Mix chocolate into creamed mixture. Spread into prepared crust. Freeze for 1 hour, or until slightly frozen. Spread with White Laced Whipped Cream to serve. Makes 8 servings.

White Laced Whipped Cream

¾ cup heavy cream
1 tablespoon powdered sugar
1 teaspoon bourbon whiskey
¼ cup chopped pecans

Combine all ingredients except pecans and beat until stiff. Spread over pie. Sprinkle top with pecans.